WITHDRAWN

W9-BMO-718

WILDERNESS

3 1526 03337123 5

12/9

EDGE BOOKS

CROSS-SECTIONS
THE M1 ABRAMS
MAIN BATTLE TANK

by Steve Parker
illustrated by Alex Pang

Capstone
press®
Mankato, Minnesota

HARFORD COUNTY
PUBLIC LIBRARY
100 E. Pennsylvania Avenue
Bel Air, MD 21014

Edge Books are published by Capstone Press, a Coughlan Publishing Company
151 Good Counsel Drive, P.O. Box 669, Mankato, Minnesota 56002.
www.capstonepress.com

Copyright © 2008 by David West Children's Books.
All rights reserved.
No part of this publication may be reproduced in whole or in part, or stored in a retrieval
system, or transmitted in any form or by any means, electronic, mechanical,
photocopying, recording, or otherwise, without written permission of the publisher.
For information regarding permission, write to Capstone Press,
151 Good Counsel Drive, P.O. Box 669, Dept. R, Mankato, Minnesota 56002.
Printed in the United States of America

Library of Congress Cataloging-in-Publication Data
Parker, Steve
    The M1 Abrams Main Battle Tank/by Steve Parker; illustrated by Alex Pang.
    p. cm.—(Edge Books. Cross-Sections)
    Includes bibliographical references and index.
    Summary: "An in-depth look at the M1 Abrams Main Battle Tank, with detailed
cross-section diagrams, action photos, and fascinating facts"—Provided by publisher.
    ISBN-13: 978-1-4296-0091-0 (hardcover)
    ISBN-10: 1-4296-0091-8 (hardcover)
    1. M1 (Tank)—Juvenile literature. 2. Tanks (Military science)—Juvenile literature.
I. Title. II. Series.
UG446.5.P347 2007
623.7'4752—dc22   2007005227

Designed and produced by

David West 🧍🧍 Children's Books
7 Princeton Court
55 Felsham Road
Putney
London SW15 1AZ

Designer: Gary Jeffrey
Editor: Gail Bushnell

Photo Credits
U. S. Army photo, 1, 13, 19; U.S. Navy photo by Photographer's Mate 1st Class
Ted Banks, 4–5; wikipedia.org, 6, 7; Sgt David Bill 48th BCT PAO, 11; PH2 Shawn
Torgerson; USN, 14; U.S. Army photo by Sgt. Kevin Bromley, 16; LCPL JAMES J.
VOORIS; USMC, 18; CWO2 Charles Grow; USMC, 20; CUMPERSGT, 21t; Staff
Sgt Aaron Allmon, 21b; DoD photo by Tech. Sgt. James Mossman, U.S. Air Force,
23; RAYMOND A. BARNARD; CIV, 24; Wakeland Kuamoo, 28; SGT PAUL L.
ANSTINE II; USMC, 23b, 29

1 2 3 4 5 6 12 11 10 09 08 07

TABLE OF CONTENTS

THE M1 ABRAMS

The M1 is the world's foremost tank. It is a heavily-armored fighting machine with a huge gun that can swivel and tilt. It can hit a target miles away. If you see U.S. tanks in the news, they are probably M1s.

Compared to most other tanks, the M1 is fast, mobile, and quiet. It is used by the U.S. Army and also the U.S. Marines, who are seen here training in California.

The M1 went into service in 1980. It has been upgraded as the M1A1 and M1A2. It is named in honor of General Creighton W. Abrams (1914–1974), former Army Chief of Staff. The M1 is also known as "The Beast," "Dracula," and "Whispering Death."

TANK HISTORY

The first tanks were built by Britain during World War I (1914–1918). They gained ground during trench warfare by advancing through barbed wire and gunfire.

Early tanks had guns on the sides to protect them against enemy fire as they crawled forward.

OVER ANY GROUND

Early tanks were called "armored land boats." Tanks have tracks which allow them to roll forward over the roughest ground. They look just like boats rolling over waves. In fact, the main body of a tank is known as the hull, as in a boat. By World War II (1939–1945), many countries used tanks in battle.

The Renault FT-17 light tank of 1917 was the first with its main gun in a rotating turret. It also had the driver in front, below the turret, and its engine at the rear. This basic layout is still used in tanks today.

HEAVY AND LIGHT

Gradually tank designs improved. Some were small, light, and fast. Heavy tanks, weighing about 50 tons (45 metric tons), were slower but better protected with bigger guns.

Germany's World War II Tiger I tanks had huge firepower and thick armor but were less mobile.

HEAVY METAL

The 1960s saw the M60 Patton as the U.S. military's Main Battle Tank, or MBT. A much improved version arrived in the late 1970s. This was gradually replaced during the early 1990s by the present U.S. MBT—the M1.

The M60 Patton had a 12-cylinder turbo-diesel engine and a road speed of about 30 miles (48 kilometers) per hour.

CROSS-SECTION

The two main parts of a tank are its body, or hull, and its swiveling top, or turret. The turret houses the main gun.

M1s have a crew of four: the commander, the driver, the gunner, and the loader, who loads the main gun with ammunition. The M1 is a heavy tank that weighs more than 40 family automobiles.

MAIN GUN
See pages 18–19

M1A2 ABRAMS
Body length: 26 feet (7.9 meters)
Width: 12 feet (3.7 meters)
Height to turret: 7 feet, 9 inches (2.4 meters)
Weight: 69.5 tons (63 metric tons)
Top speed: 42 miles (68 kilometers) per hour
Cruising range: 265 miles (426 kilometers)

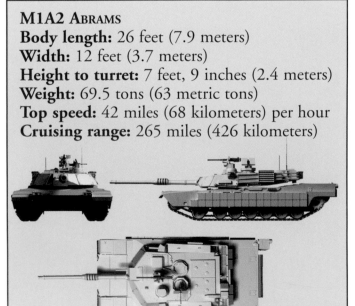

MANEUVERING
See pages
14–15

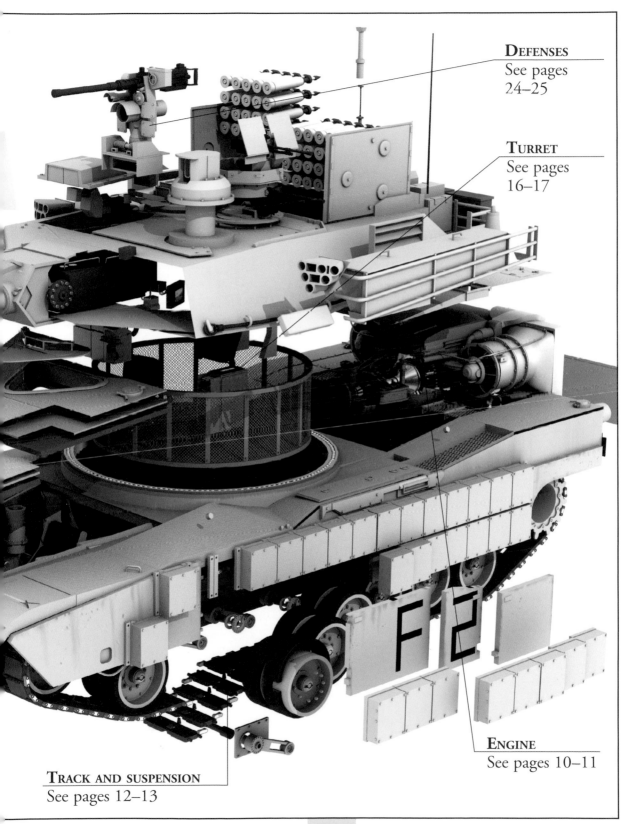

DEFENSES
See pages
24–25

TURRET
See pages
16–17

ENGINE
See pages 10–11

TRACK AND SUSPENSION
See pages 12–13

ENGINE

The M1's engine is not like a normal gasoline or diesel engine with pistons moving up and down inside cylinders. The M1's engine is a gas turbine.

ENGINE SPECIFICATIONS
AGT 1500 gas turbine
Weight: 9,065 pounds
(4,112 kilograms)
Rating: 1,500 horsepower

A gas turbine is smaller than a piston engine of the same power. It also has fewer parts. However, it uses more fuel per mile. Just starting up the M1's turbine uses 9 gallons (34 liters) of JP-8 jet fuel.

COMPRESSOR

Compressor fans squeeze the incoming air at very high pressure. The air is then mixed with fuel and burned, or combusted.

AIR INTAKE

Air is sucked into the engine by the large front fan. The air must be filtered free of sand, grit, and dirt.

TURBINE BLADES

The main turbines have angled blades like large fans. Scorching gases from burning fuel blast past them and make them spin.

EXHAUST

The exhaust gases from a turbine are very hot, so people must stay well clear. The gases also show up on the enemy's infrared (heat) sensors.

The whole turbine "pack," with its rear-facing cooling radiators, is lifted out by a crane for service and repair.

COOLING UNITS

Gas turbines work at high temperatures of more than 1,000°F (538°C). Two large cooling units remove the heat so the crew does not get too warm.

FINAL DRIVE

A system of gears takes the turning power from the main turbine's spinning shaft to the drive wheel. The drive wheel moves the track.

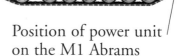

Position of power unit on the M1 Abrams

TRACK AND SUSPENSION

The M1's engine powers two drive wheels, one on each side at the rear. Each wheel has large teeth that fit into and move the track.

The 24-inch (61-centimeter) wide track lays down at the front and picks up at the back like an endless "rolling road." About 25 feet (7.6 meters) is in contact with the ground. The road wheels that run along the inside of the track give a surprisingly smooth ride.

GUIDE IDLER

The front wheel guides the track around and down onto the ground. It is turned by the track moving past.

TRACK

The T-158 track has rubber links with steel pins and connectors. A damaged link can be taken out and replaced.

ROAD WHEELS

The M1 has seven road wheels. Numbers 1, 2, and 7 have the main suspension.

The M1's gas turbine engine gives better acceleration than any other heavy tank engine. The M1 can go from 0 to 20 miles (32 kilometers) per hour in seven seconds.

DRIVE WHEEL

The single drive wheel, or drive sprocket, on each side is the only one powered by the engine.

SUSPENSION

The suspension allows the end road wheels to move up and down by about 15 inches (38 centimeters). The M1 rides over objects 3.5 feet (1 meter) high.

MANEUVERING

The driver sits low down inside the front of the tank. The body-hugging bucket seat is tilted back like a dentist's chair.

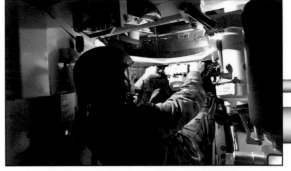

Tank drivers train in a simulator. The simulator has controls and fittings mounted in front of a computer screen.

There are only a few main controls on the M1. The steering handlebar aims the tank to the left or right. The twist-grip throttle on the handlebar speeds up the engine. The brake lever on the floor slows the tank. The driver uses periscopes to see where he is going when he is inside.

The driver raises the seat to see out whenever slow, precise maneuvering is needed.

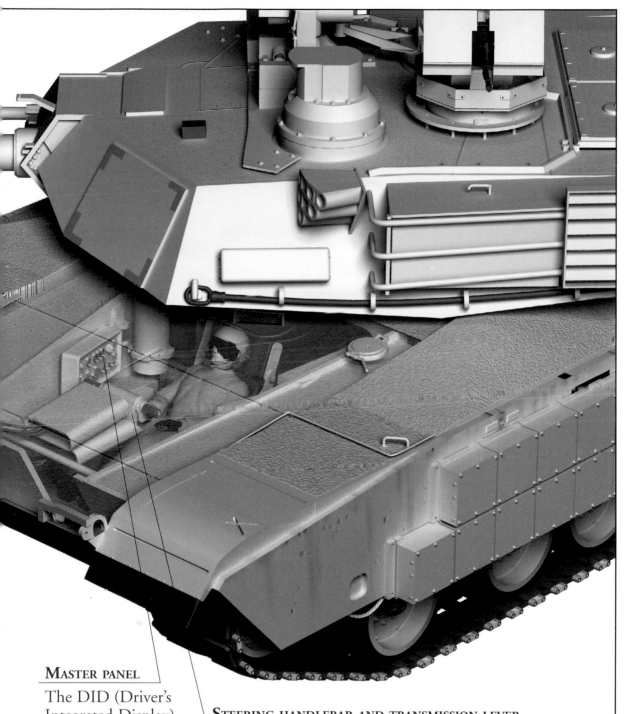

MASTER PANEL

The DID (Driver's Integrated Display) shows speed, fuel level, engine temperature, and navigation aids.

STEERING HANDLEBAR AND TRANSMISSION LEVER

Turning the handlebar operates the transmission to slow the drive wheel on one side. This drive wheel then slows the track and pulls the tank around to that side. The transmission has four forward speeds and two reverse.

TURRET CREW

The turret basket is like a revolving, electronics-packed operations room. It holds three crew members, main and smaller guns, and ammunition.

The turret, with its guns and equipment, weighs more than 26 tons (24 metric tons). Yet it can spin around in less than seven seconds. If the power fails, the turret can be turned manually.

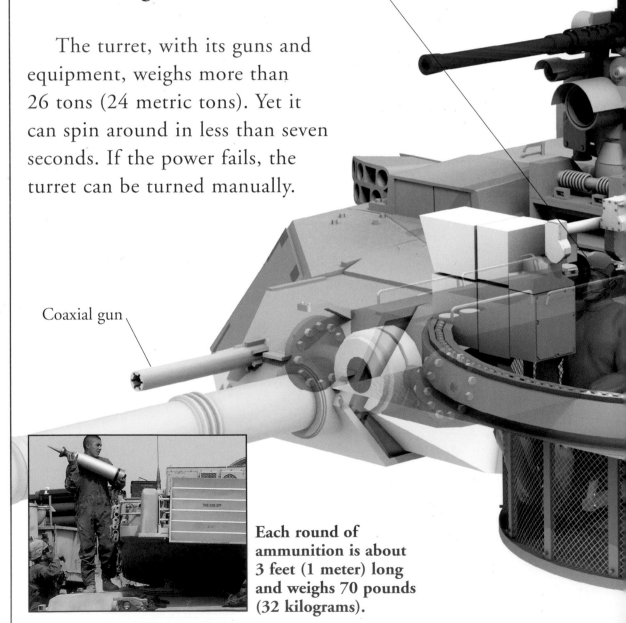

GUNNER

The gunner aims and fires the main gun and the smaller coaxial gun. The control handles, or "cadillacs," have triggers and laser buttons.

Coaxial gun

Each round of ammunition is about 3 feet (1 meter) long and weighs 70 pounds (32 kilograms).

16

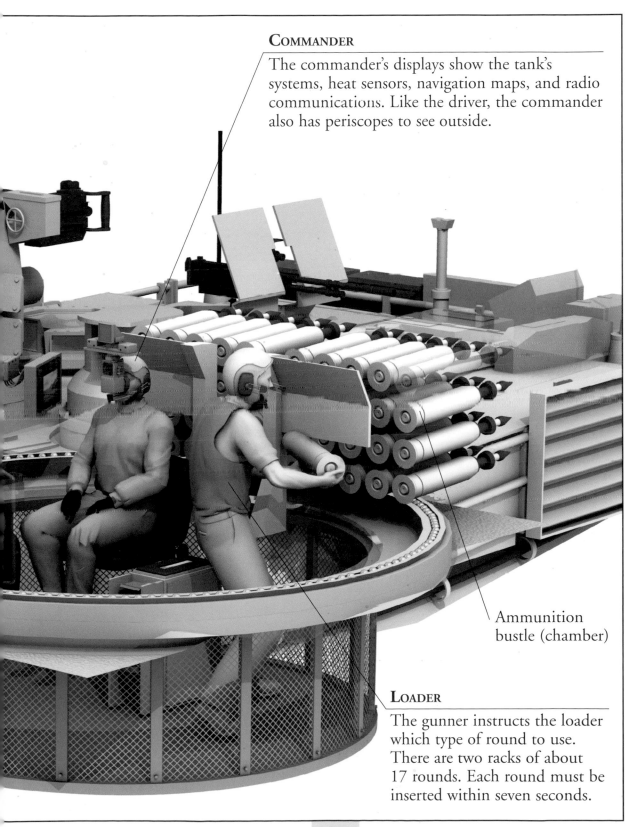

COMMANDER

The commander's displays show the tank's systems, heat sensors, navigation maps, and radio communications. Like the driver, the commander also has periscopes to see outside.

Ammunition bustle (chamber)

LOADER

The gunner instructs the loader which type of round to use. There are two racks of about 17 rounds. Each round must be inserted within seven seconds.

MAIN GUN

The M1's chief weapon is the M256 cannon. It is made by the German company, Rheinmetall, and is used on other tanks, like Leopard IIs.

At close range, the M256 cannon can smash apart a whole building.

The M256 is 120 mm caliber, meaning the hole, or bore, in the barrel is 120 mm (4.7 inches) wide. It is also a smoothbore gun. This means it lacks spiral grooves inside its barrel. Shells or bullets fired from smoothbore guns do not spin in flight.

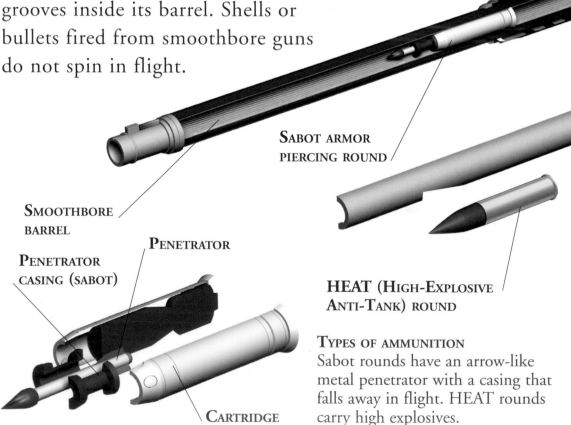

SMOOTHBORE BARREL

PENETRATOR CASING (SABOT)

PENETRATOR

CARTRIDGE

SABOT ARMOR PIERCING ROUND

HEAT (HIGH-EXPLOSIVE ANTI-TANK) ROUND

TYPES OF AMMUNITION
Sabot rounds have an arrow-like metal penetrator with a casing that falls away in flight. HEAT rounds carry high explosives.

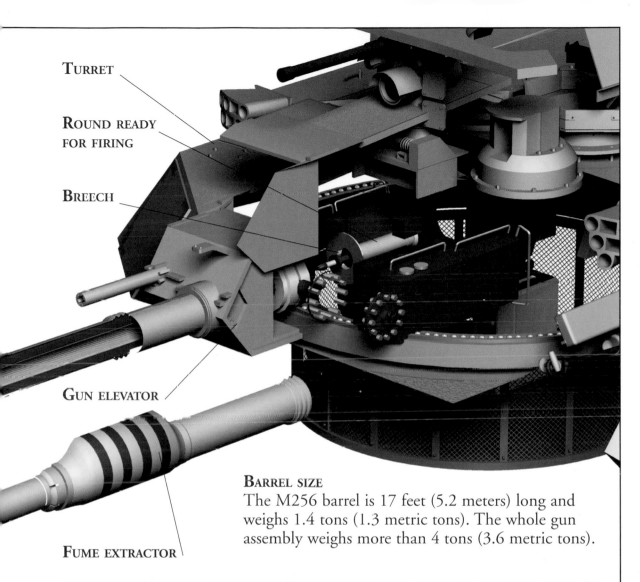

TURRET

ROUND READY
FOR FIRING

BREECH

GUN ELEVATOR

FUME EXTRACTOR

BARREL SIZE
The M256 barrel is 17 feet (5.2 meters) long and weighs 1.4 tons (1.3 metric tons). The whole gun assembly weighs more than 4 tons (3.6 metric tons).

Projectiles leave the barrel at 3,500 miles (5,630 kilometers) per hour.

ABRAMS IN ACTION

The M1 Abrams has seen action around the world. It is especially useful in open country, due to its speed and ability to cope with rough ground.

The M1 clears an area of land mines by pulling a mine plow. This plow makes the mines explode while the crew is safe.

M1s first went to battle in the Gulf War of 1991. They were better-armored and faster than Iraqi T62 and T72 tanks. The M1s scored a few direct-hit "kills" at ranges of more than 2.5 miles (4 kilometers). They were also used in Bosnia, Europe, and Afghanistan. In 2003, M1s went to Iraq for Operation Iraqi Freedom.

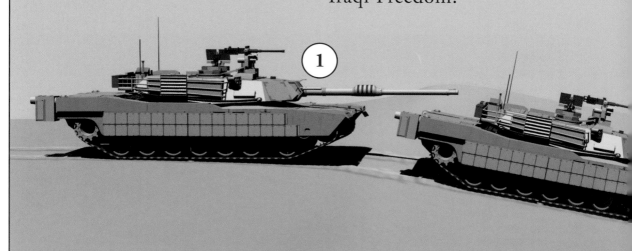

1

The Iraqi military invaded Kuwait in 1990 but retreated during the Gulf War. U.S. forces used more than 1,800 M1s.

FIRING ON THE MOVE

1. The target is out of range but the gun can lock onto it.
2. As the tank dips down a slope the automatic stabilizer tilts the gun up to keep it aimed.
3. Going up a slope, the gun tips down.
4. The laser rangefinder shows the target is near. FIRE!

The heavy armor of the M1 makes it useful for patrolling streets. The crew is protected from sniper fire and smaller explosions.

SYSTEMS

The M1 Abrams is crammed with electronics. Many systems have back-ups in case of faults or damage.

Among the main systems are viewing the surroundings by direct vision (periscopes), night-vision, and thermal sensors. The M1A2 has a Commander's Independent Thermal Viewer, or CITV. This lets the commander look for tell-tale heat from enemy equipment and automatically aim the gun at it.

The tank crew members all have headsets to communicate with each other. The headsets allow the driver in front to talk to the commander in the turret.

There are also several Global Positioning System (GPS) displays, and a sensor to show how far around the turret has swiveled on the hull. The GPS helps the crew navigate and aim weapons.

KEY TO SYSTEMS
1. Gunner's Primary Sight
2. Commander's Display Unit
3. Cross-wind Sensor
4. Commander's Internal Viewer
5. Muzzle Sensor

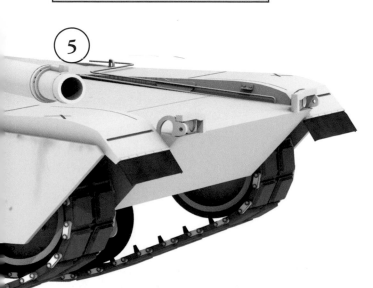

Thermal panels identify each tank to others in the dark.

DEFENSES

The M1's armor is not simply extremely thick steel. It is a series of layers, or laminates, specially designed and tested to resist all kinds of shells, bullets, and explosions.

The main armor of the M1 is known as Chobham composite armor. It has very hard ceramics, like bathroom tiles, encased in a surrounding substance, or matrix. The ceramics and matrix are sandwiched between toughened steel plates. Other defenses include three machine guns.

COAXIAL MACHINE GUN

The M240 7.62 mm machine gun is aimed and fired by the same control system as the main gun. It is mainly for use against enemy troops.

HEAVY ARMOR

The front of the turret and hull have extra-tough armor. The armor includes an extremely hard heavy metal called uranium.

This M1A1 lets off some smoke grenades as part of a training exercise.

The Browning M2 "Ma Duce" machine gun is mounted on the right of the turret, next to the commander's hatch. It can be aimed and fired by holding it directly or by remote control from inside the turret.

SAFETY AMMUNITION PANELS

The ammunition hold's top and bottom panels blow off if the tank is hit, which stops an explosion in the turret.

SMOKE GRENADES

Two sets of six smoke grenades (one set on each side) let off a big cloud of smoke. Then enemies cannot spot the tank to target it.

LOADER'S GUN SHIELD

The M240 7.62 mm machine gun next to the loader's hatch is protected by a metal shield.

REACTIVE ARMOR TILES

Reactive armor responds to an incoming weapon and blows it up a split second before it hits the tank.

THE MISSION

In modern warfare, tanks must survive against other tanks, rocket-propelled grenades, and anti-tank missiles launched from the ground, planes, and ships.

1. M1s are traveling in a convoy. They get intelligence about a brigade of enemy tanks camped to the southeast, hidden behind an oil well fire. They set off over open ground.

"Survivability" is a vital feature of the M1 Abrams. It has excellent armor. Its many sensors and detectors warn of danger and incoming enemy weapons. The crew has time to react and stay safe.

4. The gunner grips the trigger—BOOM! The armor-piercing sabot round penetrates the enemy tank, spraying molten uranium inside the turret. Fires start and ammunition explodes as the enemy tank is destroyed.

2. An M1 hits a mine which blows its track off, but the crew is unharmed. The rest of the M1s keep aim as they speed across the rough ground.

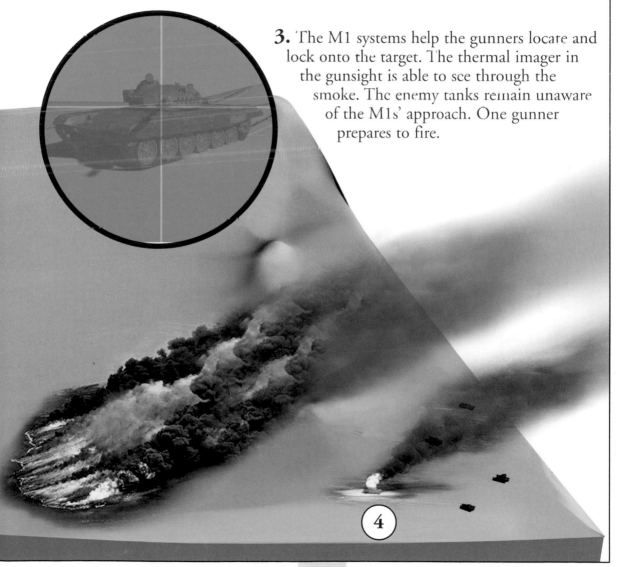

3. The M1 systems help the gunners locate and lock onto the target. The thermal imager in the gunsight is able to see through the smoke. The enemy tanks remain unaware of the M1s' approach. One gunner prepares to fire.

4

THE FUTURE

The M1 Abrams is more than 25 years old. Can it continue its success?

More than 8,800 M1s have been built for U.S. forces. The latest M1A2s are so improved from the original M1s that they are

Older M1s are re-equipped with new electronics, better sensors and imagers, and improved communications. There is also a newer LV100-5 turbine engine.

almost new tanks. About 1,000 of the older U.S. M1s are being upgraded to the latest M1A2 designs. This successful M1A2 design is not due to be fully replaced until 2030.

Some experts say that tanks will have little use in the future. They think battles will involve mainly remote-controlled missiles, perhaps even in space. But others say the M1 Abrams will spearhead the U.S. Army for years to come.

New ammunition includes M1028 120-mm anti-personnel canisters. These M1028s are used for fighting in close quarters and knocking small holes in buildings.

A few M1s are still being produced for other countries. Different versions of the M1 have been sold to Egypt, Kuwait, Saudi Arabia, and Australia.

GLOSSARY

armor (AR-mur)—a protective metal covering

exhaust (eg-ZAWST)—very hot gases leaving an engine

gas turbine (GAS TUR-byne)—a type of engine that works by hot gases spinning a turbine with fanlike blades

horsepower (HORSS-pou-ur)—the measurement of an engine's power, abbreviated as hp

hull (HUL)—the main body of a tank or similar armored vehicle

infrared (in-fruh-RED)—able to find objects by picking up traces of heat

suspension (suss-PEN-shun)—the tilting arms, springs, dampers, and other parts that smooth out road bumps so a vehicle's ride is more comfortable

track (TRAK)—on a tank or tracked vehicle, the links that form an endless loop, like a conveyor belt or "rolling road"

transmission (trans-MISH-uhn)—gears and other parts that transfer the power from the engine to the wheels

READ MORE

Cornish, Geoff. *Tanks.* Military Hardware in Action. Minneapolis: Lerner, 2003.

Green, Michael, and Gladys Green. *Main Battle Tanks: The M1A1 Abrams.* War Machines. Mankato, Minn.: Capstone Press, 2004.

Souter, Gerry. *Battle Tanks: Power in the Field.* Berkeley Heights, N.J.: Enslow, 2006.

INTERNET SITES

FactHound offers a safe, fun way to find Internet sites related to this book. All of the sites on FactHound have been researched by our staff.

Here's how:
1. Visit *www.facthound.com*
2. Choose your grade level.
3. Type in this book ID **1429600918** for age-appropriate sites. You may also browse subjects by clicking on letters, or by clicking on pictures and words.
4. Click on the **Fetch It** button.

FactHound will fetch the best sites for you!

INDEX